Growing in Self-Esteem

BY MARIE PAUL CURLEY, FSP

PAULINE
BOOKS & MEDIA

Boston

Library of Congress Control Number: 2023939036

ISBN 10: 0-8198-1691-4
ISBN 13: 978-0-8198-1691-7

Cover design by Tisa Muico

Published by Pauline Books & Media, 50 Saint Pauls Avenue, Boston, MA 02130-3491

Printed in the U.S.A.

www.pauline.org

Pauline Books & Media is the publishing house of the Daughters of St. Paul, an international congregation of women religious serving the Church with the communications media.

1 2 3 4 5 6 7 8 9   30 29 28 27 26 25 24

Contents

Introduction

When I was ten or eleven years old, I knew that I lacked self-confidence. At the time, I had no idea what self-esteem was, but I felt imprisoned by feelings of self-doubt and fear. Thankfully, every Sunday when my family attended Mass, two of my parish priests preached repeatedly about God's love. Their words challenged how I thought about myself and about God.

During my difficult early teen years, one thought resisted my self-doubt and looming hopelessness—the possibility that God loved me, or that at least God might eventually love me. My hope in this possibility eventually gave me the courage to follow my vocation in the religious life, despite serious doubts about my self-worth. Gradually, I started to believe what my faith, the word of God, trusted mentors, and my experiences in prayer told me— God truly loves me! And God loves *you* too!

You may wonder if self-esteem is something that a person of faith should care about. You may have heard that followers of Christ don't need self-esteem because they are supposed to be selfless. But growing in a healthy self-esteem is not about being selfish. A healthy self-esteem allows us to embrace God's will for our lives and to live life with more joy.

Perhaps you have been haunted by a lack of self-esteem that has even, at times, completely debilitated you at important moments in life's journey. Lacking a healthy view of self can easily lead to self-hate, self-loathing, and even self-destructive behavior. It can be hard—sometimes impossible—to love others selflessly when we don't love ourselves and know our own worth.

Do you know your own worth?

I know how it feels not to know my own worth. But over time, God's love has become the bedrock of my self-esteem, my life, and my joy. God's love for me enables me to love others more deeply. The happiness, strength, and peace that comes from knowing God's love can transform your life too. These treasures can grow in you.

The Bible tells us in countless ways that God loves us. Praying with and meditating on the word of God has become my daily path for living in the light of God's love. I am excited to share this little collection of Scripture passages followed by reflections based on my experience in growing in self-esteem. I hope and pray that they will help you come to know just how much God loves and cherishes you!

1

God Chose to Create You

O LORD, you have searched me and known me.
For it was you who formed my inward parts;
    you knit me together in my mother's womb.
I praise you, for I am fearfully and wonderfully made.
    Wonderful are your works;
that I know very well.

PSALM 139:1, 13–14

There is one truth that cannot be twisted no matter how much wounded human nature might try—God chose to create you. God *wants* to share his life with you. God wants you in the world.

You may feel convinced deep down that you are no good, that there is something fundamentally wrong with you. But God, who is all-wise and all-good, created you as you are, with your personality and potential. God lovingly created you and sustains you. This reality is bedrock upon which you can build a new foundation for a positive sense of self-worth.

O God, you made everything (including me!) and indeed, it is very good (see Genesis 1:31). Thank you for giving me life. I trust your love that holds me in being at every moment.

2

God Will Never Forget You

Zion said, "The LORD has forsaken me,
    my Lord has forgotten me."
Can a woman forget her nursing child,
    or show no compassion for the child of her womb?
Even these may forget,
    yet I will not forget you.

ISAIAH 49:14–15

God's love is the model for all human love, not the other way around. Love between humans is merely a faint likeness of God's astonishingly faithful and completely unconditional love. Nevertheless, we often base our ideas of God's love on the love we received (or did not receive) from our parents, family, or friends.

Perhaps at times you have doubted God's love because of the way someone has treated you. But in the moments when you doubt God's love, remember—God will never forget his love for you. When you feel the pain of rejection or abuse, or the limitations of another person's love, you can remind yourself that God does not reject you. God understands you and is tenderly faithful. God will always be at your side. Jesus' entire life, but especially his passion, death, and resurrection, is constant proof that God is faithful and will *never* abandon you.

Lord, your love for me is trustworthy and reliable. When the pain of rejection and abandonment wells up in me, help me to trust in your promise: "I will never forget you."

3

God Never Makes Mistakes

Bless the LORD, O my soul,
>   and do not forget all his benefits—
The LORD is merciful and gracious,
>   slow to anger and abounding in steadfast love.
He does not deal with us according to our sins,
>   nor repay us according to our iniquities.
For as the heavens are high above the earth,
>   so great is his steadfast love toward those who fear
>   him;
as far as the east is from the west,
>   so far he removes our transgressions from us.

PSALM 103:2, 8, 10–12

Do you see your mistakes and sometimes count them as evidence that you are worthless and no good? At times like this, you can remember that God does not see your mistakes as an insurmountable problem. God's mercy is much bigger than any mistake. God is not, as some may imagine, like a judge in an Olympic competition. God does not give marks for your performance, scrutinize mistakes, and replay them from every angle.

God—the only one who doesn't make mistakes—is your Creator. You could never, ever *be* a mistake. You may *make* mistakes, but God is bigger than your mistakes. Your mistakes can become reminders that God loves you no matter what. Mistakes are opportunities to learn and to lean on God. At the deepest core of your being, God loves you unconditionally. God is always gazing lovingly into your heart.

O Lord, thank you for loving me with all my flaws and fragility. I believe in your love for me. I trust that no matter what, your grace can renew my life.

4

God Can Fulfill Your Needs

My God, my God, why have you forsaken me?
>Why are you so far from helping me, from the
>words of my groaning?
>. . . O my help, come quickly to my aid!
>Save me from the mouth of the lion!
From the horns of the wild oxen you have rescued me.
You who fear the LORD, praise him! . . .
For he did not despise or abhor
>the affliction of the afflicted;
he did not hide his face from me,
>but heard when I cried to him.

PSALM 22:1, 19, 21, 23, 24

Neediness is part of being human. Though it can be distressing, having unfulfilled needs is normal. Instead of blaming yourself for your needs, acknowledge your needs and entrust your neediness to God.

On the cross, Jesus uses the words of Psalm 22 to entrust himself into the loving hands of the Father. You,

9

too, can entrust your needs to God and discover that God's love *is* enough. God's love embraces you—circling, sustaining, cradling. Living in God's love will give you the courage to use your God-given gifts and trust that God will provide for all your needs.

My God, sometimes I feel so empty, so lonely. Fill my heart with your love and help me to believe that your love is all that I need.

5

You Are Called by God

Consider your own call, brothers and sisters: not many of you were wise by human standards, not many were powerful, not many were of noble birth. But God chose what is foolish in the world to shame the wise; God chose what is weak in the world to shame the strong; God chose what is low and despised in the world, things that are not, to reduce to nothing things that are, so that no one might boast in the presence of God. He is the source of your life in Christ Jesus.

1 Corinthians 1:26–30

All of us—even great saints—have reasons to feel inadequate. Feelings of inadequacy can make us forget that being called by God is not about being worthy. It is about being loved. None of us are worthy of our sacred baptismal vocation to be Christ for others.

Whatever your vocation, whether it is to give your spouse and children a foundational experience of unconditional love, or to dedicate yourself single-heartedly to promoting the dignity of human life, or to serve in ministry—you are called by God to do something unique with your life and gifts.

You don't have to worry about feeling worthy or comparing yourself to others. All you have to do is simply acknowledge who has called you and trust in the power of Christ's grace and mercy.

O Lord, your love creates goodness in me, for you love me into being. When you call me to use my gifts, help me to trust in you!

6

You Don't Need to Prove Yourself

"Look at the birds of the air; they neither sow nor reap nor gather into barns, and yet your heavenly Father feeds them. Are you not of more value than they? And can any of you by worrying add a single hour to your span of life? And why do you worry about clothing? Consider the lilies of the field, how they grow; they neither toil nor spin, yet I tell you, even Solomon in all his glory was not clothed like one of these. But if God so clothes the grass of the field, which is alive today and tomorrow is thrown into the oven, will he not much more clothe you—you of little faith?"

MATTHEW 6:26–30

It's so easy to fall into the trap of trying to prove ourselves through achievements. But when we begin to trust in God's love for us, we can also entrust the results of our efforts to his loving care. What we do is important, but the results of our efforts are not up to us. They are up to God.

God has a plan for you and is always working for your good. And God's plan is always better than anything you could come up with. God does not need you to prove yourself. God already loves you. When you allow this fact to root your life, it can give your daily efforts a sense of security and peace.

O God, when I am tempted to think I must prove myself, help me to believe that you already love me and take great delight in who I am. Thank you for your love!

7

God Can Free You from Fear

God's love was revealed among us in this way: God sent his only Son into the world so that we might live through him. In this is love, not that we loved God but that he loved us and sent his Son to be the atoning sacrifice for our sins. Beloved, since God loved us so much, we also ought to love one another. . . . God is love, and those who abide in love abide in God, and God abides in them. There is no fear in love, but perfect love casts out fear.

1 JOHN 4:9–11, 16, 18

Fighting to be "good enough" is a self-defeating and never-ending vicious circle. It leads to self-absorption and distraction from the real purpose of life. On the other hand, each time we choose to act for the love of God, self, or neighbor, we take a step away from being controlled by fear and a step toward greater love and freedom.

Are you sometimes driven by the fear of not being good enough—in your own eyes, in the eyes of others, or perhaps even in the eyes of God? God's love can free you from this fear. You can reinforce healthy self-esteem by allowing your choices to reflect the conviction that you are loved, instead of fearing what others might say or think. Living in God's love has the power to destroy your fear and fill you with the joy of Christ.

Lord, help me to experience the powerful love that you have for me so that I can let go of fear and truly trust in your love, which always leads me closer to you.

8

God Wants You to Be Honest

Someone from the crowd answered [Jesus], "Teacher, I brought you my son; he has a spirit that makes him unable to speak. . . . It has often cast him into the fire and into the water, to destroy him; but if you are able to do anything, have pity on us and help us." Jesus said to him, "If you are able!—All things can be done for the one who believes." Immediately the father of the child cried out, "I believe; help my unbelief!" When Jesus saw that a crowd came running together, he rebuked the unclean spirit, saying to it, "You spirit that keeps this boy from speaking and hearing, I command you, come out of him, and never enter him again!"

MARK 9:17, 22–26

When reading the Gospels attentively, you may have noticed that Jesus responds readily to honesty in his interactions with people. Even when people challenge him, Jesus seems to appreciate those who speak from the heart. You may think that your prayer needs to come from the best part of yourself—the part that is *not* angry or jealous or fearful. But God wants your prayer to come from your entire being.

God wants you to share everything with him—every feeling, every experience, and every fear. Try speaking to God honestly from your heart today. You will see that God cannot resist responding. Your prayer will become a holy and intimate dialogue: from your heart to God's, and from God's heart to yours.

Jesus, sometimes I avoid sharing the messiness of my interior life with you because I fear showing you my real self. Help me to trust and confide everything to you.

9

When You Doubt God's Love

If God is for us, who is against us? He who did not withhold his own Son, but gave him up for all of us, will he not with him also give us everything else? Who will separate us from the love of Christ? Will hardship, or distress, or persecution, or famine, or nakedness, or peril, or sword?

No, in all these things we are more than conquerors through him who loved us. For I am convinced that neither death, nor life, nor angels, nor rulers, nor things present, nor things to come, nor powers, nor height, nor depth, nor anything else in all creation, will be able to separate us from the love of God in Christ Jesus our Lord.

Romans 8:31–32, 35, 37–39

What if we really believed this exultant conclusion to Saint Paul's hymn to God's love? When we are feeling anxious, life can seem like an endless series of obstacles. But what if life were not a series of obstacles but a series of opportunities through which we discover God's faithful love anew?

Whenever doubts arise about whether God loves you, you can stop by a church for a visit. A tangible pledge of God's ever-faithful love is Jesus' Presence in the Eucharist. Try praying to Jesus in the tabernacle or attend Mass and consider God's self-giving love. Prayer will help you to realize just how much God loves you. Nothing can separate you from God's love.

Jesus, I believe you are present in the Holy Eucharist in your Body, Blood, soul, and divinity. In the Eucharist, you long to heal today, just like you healed people while you lived on earth. Heal me too!

10

Your Fragility Is Blessed

But we have this treasure in clay jars, so that it may be made clear that this extraordinary power belongs to God and does not come from us. We are afflicted in every way, but not crushed. . . . For while we live, we are always being given up to death for Jesus' sake, so that the life of Jesus may be made visible in our mortal flesh.

So we do not lose heart. Even though our outer nature is wasting away, our inner nature is being renewed day by day. For this slight momentary affliction is preparing us for an eternal weight of glory beyond all measure.

2 CORINTHIANS 4:7–8, 11, 16–17

Saint Paul's image of the treasure held in a fragile clay jar perfectly captures the paradox of life in Christ: the immensity of each person's call and our littleness in the face of it. This wonderful image is one key to understanding the essential virtue of humility.

Christian literature from earlier times is sometimes misunderstood as promoting a humility that is at odds with healthy self-esteem. But humility is a foundation for self-esteem because this virtue is a clear recognition of the truth about yourself and God. All human beings are frail, liable to fall and shatter in an instant. Yet your fragility is astoundingly blessed with God's graced invitations. Humility is the virtue that can enable you to dare to accept both your fragility and the splendid treasures that God gives you.

Lord, help me to understand that by knowing my own frailty and weakness, I will witness your strength. Relying on your strength, I can do great things and give you the glory.

11

You Are Lovable

One of the scribes came near and heard them disputing with one another, and seeing that he answered them well, he asked him, "Which commandment is the first of all?" Jesus answered, "The first is, 'Hear, O Israel: the Lord our God, the Lord is one; you shall love the Lord your God with all your heart, and with all your soul, and with all your mind, and with all your strength.' The second is this, 'You shall love your neighbor as yourself.' There is no other commandment greater than these."

MARK 12:28–31

Does self-hatred prevent you from receiving God's love in its fullness and fully living your unique calling? God wants you to be a source of peace and love for others, by accepting and loving yourself for who you are. God calls you to be rooted in love, and this includes a healthy love of self.

Without a healthy self-love, the command of Jesus to love your neighbors as yourself makes no sense at all. You can begin to genuinely love yourself by being gentle with yourself. What if you could see yourself through God's eyes? Under God's gaze, you will come to understand your identity as a child of God, created and loved. You were chosen to be Christ's dwelling place *and* for a particular mission of service. You are indeed lovable.

Jesus, when I am harsh with myself, I am also harsh with others. Help me to be gentler with myself so that I can be gentle with others. Let me reflect your love to them.

12

Jesus' Invitation to You

When they had finished breakfast, Jesus said to Simon Peter, "Simon son of John, do you love me more than these?" He said to him, "Yes, Lord; you know that I love you." Jesus said to him, "Feed my lambs." A second time he said to him, "Simon son of John, do you love me?" He said to him, "Yes, Lord; you know that I love you." Jesus said to him, "Tend my sheep." He said to him the third time, "Simon son of John, do you love me?" Peter felt hurt because he said to him the third time, "Do you love me?" And he said to him, "Lord, you know everything; you know that I love you." Jesus said to him, "Feed my sheep."

JOHN 21:15–17

Peter was full of shame and self-doubt after he denied Jesus not once but three times. But in this intimate breakfast scene in the Gospel of John, Peter confidently and immediately renewed his commitment to Jesus. What was Peter's secret? He acknowledged his own sinfulness, but he also focused on the mercy and grace of God.

Peter knew that God has an amazing way of bringing something good out of everything, even sin. Though Peter had failed Jesus terribly, he remembered Jesus' love for him. Jesus invites you to do the same. God knows you better than you could ever know yourself, and even knowing your sinfulness, God will never abandon you.

Jesus, I believe that you look at me with love. Accept my love in return. Help me to focus not on my weakness, but on your love and mercy.

13

God's Inexhaustible Mercy

Jesus said, "There was a man who had two sons. The younger of them said to his father, 'Father, give me the share of the property that will belong to me.' . . . [The younger son] squandered his property in dissolute living. When he had spent everything, a severe famine took place throughout that country, and he began to be in need. . . . So he set off and went to his father. But while he was still far off, his father saw him and was filled with compassion; he ran and put his arms around him and kissed him. 'Quickly, bring out a robe—the best one—and put it on him; put a ring on his finger and sandals on his feet. And get the fatted calf and kill it and let us eat and celebrate; for this son of mine was dead and is alive again; he was lost and is found!'"

Luke 15:11–14, 20, 22–24

Each time we become more aware of our sinfulness and seek forgiveness, we have an opportunity to grow closer to God. God never tires of bringing us new life!

God offers us healing and forgiveness through the sacrament of Reconciliation, the celebration of God's inexhaustible mercy and a renewal of relationship with God.

In the ocean of God's mercy, your shame and sinfulness become insignificant and are washed away. God's forgiveness means that your guilt does not have the last word.

Jesus, you told the apostles, "If you forgive the sins of any, they are forgiven them" (John 20:23). I thank you for the amazing gift of the sacrament of Reconciliation. Help me to receive it often.

14

God Works in Your Life

[Solomon prayed], ". . . O Lord my God, you have made your servant king in place of my father David, although I am only a little child; I do not know how to go out or come in. And your servant is in the midst of the people whom you have chosen, a great people, so numerous they cannot be numbered or counted. Give your servant therefore an understanding mind to govern your people, able to discern between good and evil."

1 Kings 3:7–9

Humility is to be in right relationship with yourself, God, and others. To be humble includes knowing and accepting who you really are; acknowledging your utter dependence on God; and being responsible for your choices and actions, striving to be fair and kind both to yourself and others.

Growing in self-awareness is an important part of humility. A spiritual practice called the examen of consciousness is one way to become more self-aware. The examen is a prayerful review of the events of your day, looking at both the graces you received and how you responded to them. The examen and the virtue of humility can help you to have a healthy self-esteem that is firmly rooted in truth. When the examen is done regularly, it can help you to become increasingly aware of how God works in your life and in the choices you make.

Lord, you know me better than I know myself. Please give me the light of the Holy Spirit so that I may grow in self-knowledge and use that knowledge to love you and others more.

15

Cultivate a Grateful Heart

It is good to give thanks to the LORD,
    to sing praises to your name, O Most High;
to declare your steadfast love in the morning,
    and your faithfulness by night.
For you, O LORD, have made me glad by your work;
    at the works of your hands I sing for joy.

PSALM 92:1–2, 4

Life can seem like an enormous burden, not a gift, especially when we are struggling with any kind of deep pain, including low self-esteem or self-hatred. Cultivating a grateful heart in these circumstances can be really hard work. Living in a spirit of thanksgiving is not easy, particularly when we are suffering.

Painful times contain hidden blessings. In times of suffering or hardship, it helps to remember the good that God faithfully gives you every day—the gift of existence, the ability to be self-aware and to make choices, and the capacity to experience love and joy, even when life is painful. As you practice becoming more aware of the gift of each moment, your joy and awareness of God's loving care for you will deepen too.

Dear Lord, please give me the strength and courage to live this day with serenity. Thank you for the gift of my life and for your loving care. May I always give thanks for your incredible love.

16

God Wants to Surprise You

"Ask, and it will be given to you; search, and you will find; knock, and the door will be opened for you. For everyone who asks receives, and everyone who searches finds, and for everyone who knocks, the door will be opened."

LUKE 11:9–10

Jesus wants us to trust him with our wants and needs because God delights in providing for us. But just as we can be disappointed by someone we trust, sometimes we may also feel disappointed in God. The anger and hurt that accompany disappointment may be hard to cope with initially, but if we close ourselves off completely from hope, we risk becoming less receptive to the unexpected ways that God may want to grace us.

Have you ever prayed for something and not received it? How did you feel? Unfulfilled longings are a reminder that you are incomplete, that you need God. Having

needs and desires is a part of being human and sharing
them with another is an act of trust. When you are able
to accept your emptiness, you make room for the sur-
prises God wants to give you.

*Dear God, help me to find contentment by aligning my will
with yours so I can say with your Son, Jesus, "Not my will but
yours be done" (Luke 22:42). I trust you want the best for me.*

17

Perfectionism Is a Myth

Trust in the LORD, and do good;
    so you will live in the land, and enjoy security.
Take delight in the LORD,
    and he will give you the desires of your heart.
Commit your way to the LORD;
    trust in him, and he will act.
He will make your vindication shine like the light
    and the justice of your cause like the noonday.
Be still before the LORD, and wait patiently for him.

PSALM 37:3–7

Perfectionism is a myth. While God makes many promises in Scripture, he never promises perfection. No matter how hard we try, we will never be perfect in this life. God always has our best interests at heart. He cares less about efficiency and results and more about our growth in faith and trust. To see a situation from God's perspective can help us escape perfectionism.

When you feel lost in perfectionism, you may be surprised to discover how helpful it is to seek the bigger picture. God is your greatest security. You can cling to God the Almighty who is your Creator, Provider, Merciful Redeemer, and Beginning and End.

Dear Lord, if I trust in you, I will never be disappointed. Help me to trust in your never-ending love and Providence in my life.

18

God Works through Your Weakness

A thorn was given me in the flesh, a messenger of Satan to torment me, to keep me from being too elated. Three times I appealed to the Lord about this, that it would leave me, but he said to me, "My grace is sufficient for you, for power is made perfect in weakness."

2 Corinthians 12:7–9

Have you ever prayed to God to free you from your vulnerability? Like Saint Paul, you probably know what it is like to want to be free of your weaknesses. When you feel like this, it is important to remember that while Paul felt burdened by his weakness, he also recognized that God wanted to work through his limitations. Weaknesses help you to see clearly that you aren't in control. Your weaknesses provide space for God to draw near and take over.

Our God, who has no limitations, *rejoices* when you invite him into your life to use the very weaknesses you want to cast aside. If God can rejoice in working through your weaknesses, then you no longer need to let them bother you! Instead, you can accept your limitations and entrust them to God. You may think your weaknesses are shadows, but it is in these very shadows that Jesus delights in shining the most brilliant light.

Jesus, I believe that your grace is sufficient for me, like it was for Saint Paul. You always sustain me despite my weaknesses. Help me to accept my limitations as well as my gifts.

19

Fix Your Gaze on Jesus

Let us also lay aside every weight and the sin that clings so closely, and let us run with perseverance the race that is set before us, looking to Jesus the pioneer and perfecter of our faith, who for the sake of the joy that was set before him endured the cross, disregarding its shame, and has taken his seat at the right hand of the throne of God.

HEBREWS 12:1–2

When your gaze is focused on yourself or on the difficult areas of your life, Christ is excluded from your line of sight. But with God's grace, you can learn to center your gaze on God and glimpse the deeper meaning and beauty in your life.

Focusing on God's love can open up the true landscape of life. You can discover the beauty of Christ's presence by directing your inner gaze toward God, who already fills your life. When you center yourself on Jesus, you welcome God's grace. Opening yourself to God's grace allows you to see him in others and make decisions that are more loving and life-giving. God's love in Christ can completely transform your life if you let it.

Lord Jesus, help me to focus on your presence within me. What a mystery—that through grace you dwell in me! Help me to live in this mystery throughout my day.

20

Your Life Is in God's Hands

"Abide in me as I abide in you. Just as the branch cannot bear fruit by itself unless it abides in the vine, neither can you unless you abide in me. I am the vine, you are the branches. Those who abide in me and I in them bear much fruit, because apart from me you can do nothing. If you abide in me, and my words abide in you, ask for whatever you wish, and it will be done for you. My Father is glorified by this, that you bear much fruit and become my disciples."

JOHN 15:4–5, 7–8

Jesus didn't say, "Apart from me you can do *some things*." But let's face it—most of us interpret his words this way in our practical, everyday lives. What if you truly began to act in the truth that *everything* you seek to do, every aspect of your life, is ultimately in God's hands?

While it can be terrifying to admit how limited, vulnerable, and powerless you are, your powerlessness is only a small part of the picture. You are continually sustained by a loving God. When you discover and accept your unique place in the plan of God, you will find unimaginable freedom. Jesus offers you that freedom today.

Lord Jesus, apart from you I can do nothing. But with your help, I can do all you call me to do, even great things. Sustain me with that hope so that my life may be wholly directed to you.

21

Be True to Yourself

For in Christ Jesus neither circumcision nor uncircumcision counts for anything; the only thing that counts is faith working through love.

You were running well; who prevented you from obeying the truth? Such persuasion does not come from the one who calls you. A little yeast leavens the whole batch of dough. . . .

For you were called to freedom, brothers and sisters; only do not use your freedom as an opportunity for self-indulgence, but through love become slaves to one another. For the whole law is summed up in a single commandment, "You shall love your neighbor as yourself."

GALATIANS 5:6–9, 13–14

Do you feel free to speak and act from the core of your identity, rather than from a false sense of guilt, obligation, or entanglement? The freer you are, the more fully you can engage in authentic relationships and serve the Lord at the same time. Healthy relationships allow you to respond to another person's needs while at the same time maintaining your own identity and taking care of your own concerns. You are called to make a gift of yourself to others—a gift that only you can give! But becoming a gift for others does not involve putting their priorities before God's. Finding this balance is difficult, but in it you will find freedom.

Dear God, I want to be generous, but sometimes I do more than I feel I can and sometimes less. Help me to find a balance by living in your love.

22

God Draws Close to the Suffering

When the righteous cry for help, the LORD hears,
    and rescues them from all their troubles.
The LORD is near to the brokenhearted,
    and saves the crushed in spirit.
Many are the afflictions of the righteous,
    but the LORD rescues them from them all.
He keeps all their bones;
    not one of them will be broken.

PSALM 34:17–20

Psalm 34 offers an extraordinary expression of faith and reveals many things about God. For one, God is particularly *near* to the brokenhearted. God is with us, his people, in a special way when we suffer.

God pays special attention to those devastated by suffering. And God also calls you, as a person of faith, to try to alleviate others' suffering. But when you feel overwhelmed by the scope of a tragedy, this can be difficult. You might feel a natural tendency to run away when you

45

are confronted with another's suffering that you cannot alleviate.

God, however, does the opposite. God draws close. Faith doesn't take away the mystery or the suffering but offers another mystery—that God does not run from those who suffer. He draws near.

Lord, help me to unite my suffering with yours for the salvation of souls and the good of others. Suffering is such a mystery, but you suffered for us on the cross, and I believe in your promise of eternal life.

23

Your Vocation to Love

"I give you a new commandment, that you love one another. Just as I have loved you, you also should love one another. By this everyone will know that you are my disciples, if you have love for one another."

JOHN 13:34–35

Jesus said that the second of the two greatest commandments is "love your neighbor as yourself" (Matthew 22:39). This is a striking command, and the phrase that many of us overlook is "as yourself." These two words can be the key to understanding this commandment.

Jesus says that in order to love others, you have to know how to truly love yourself. True love of self has nothing to do with being selfish. Loving yourself begins with respecting your dignity as a child of God, your individuality, your ability to think, your free will to

47

choose, and your vocation to love. Loving one another includes many elements—support, compassion, understanding, and self-sacrifice. But the strength of any relationship between two people is founded primarily on respect. To respect and love others as they deserve, you need to first respect and love yourself as God loves you. If you are not sure how to begin loving yourself, ask God for help. He will teach you.

Lord Jesus, thank you for making me who I am. Help me to reject any form of self-hatred and to love myself in the proper way. Enable me to respect others and to see your image in them.

24

Forgiveness Will Free You

"Pray then in this way:
Our Father in heaven,
    hallowed be your name.
    Your kingdom come.
    Your will be done,
        on earth as it is in heaven.
    Give us this day our daily bread.
    And forgive us our debts,
        as we also have forgiven our debtors.
    And do not bring us to the time of trial,
        but rescue us from the evil one.
For if you forgive others their trespasses, your
    heavenly Father will also forgive you."

Matthew 6:9–14

The journey to forgiveness is graced and mysterious. It often happens piece by piece—a gradual letting go that begins with a simple desire to be healed. Genuine forgiveness involves honesty about what happened, respect for the dignity of all involved, and acceptance of the human condition.

If you are struggling to forgive, it's important to remember that the ability to forgive goes beyond the ordinary powers of the human heart. God will give the grace. In the meantime, you can learn to live in the truth that you are forgiven. As you experience God's mercy in your life, it will help you to discern the difference between moving toward forgiveness in honesty and truth, and fostering unhealthy resentment. Forgiveness doesn't stop the pain. But it will free you from the shadows of the past and empower you to move into the future, open to new life.

Father, "forgive us our trespasses as we forgive those who trespass against us." When I find it hard to forgive, change my heart, Lord, so that I can let go of hurts and find inner freedom.

25

God Always Helps You to Grow

Whatever gains I had, these I have come to regard as loss because of Christ. More than that, I regard everything as loss because of the surpassing value of knowing Christ Jesus my Lord. For his sake I have suffered the loss of all things, and I regard them as rubbish, in order that I may gain Christ and be found in him.

PHILIPPIANS 3:7–9

After Paul's conversion, gaining Christ was all that mattered to him. He had discovered the amazing power of God that raised Jesus from the dead—transforming Jesus' death into resurrection. And Paul knew that God's transforming power was also at work in his own life, even in suffering and death. God's amazing love continually "makes the best" of human sinfulness. Only the awesome power of God can bring good out of the malevolence of sin. Out of the vindictive execution of his Son, God brought Christ's resurrection and the salvation of humanity.

God dearly loves you, and for this reason he is constantly making the best of your life. Even when you suffer, even when you sin, God uses that pain or sinful choice to help you to grow and to draw nearer to Christ. Life in Christ doesn't take away the suffering that is part of human existence, but it does transform it.

Dear God, you freely give us grace because your Son, Jesus, gave his life for us. When I have anything to suffer, help me to offer it in union with Jesus so that I can become more like your Son.

26

God Wants to Be Your Light

I saw the holy city, the new Jerusalem, coming down out of heaven from God. . . . I saw no temple in the city, for its temple is the Lord God the Almighty and the Lamb. And the city has no need of sun or moon to shine on it, for the glory of God is its light, and its lamp is the Lamb. The nations will walk by its light. . . . Its gates will never be shut by day—and there will be no night there.

REVELATION 21:2, 22–25

Life is filled with beacons of light that can guide you to your desired destination. In dark times, however, you may feel unsure how to get to a place free from fear, a place with meaning and purpose. When you are immersed in the depths of a profound darkness, God's light seems absent.

Whether your life is stormy or sunny right now, what or who you choose to guide you will make a radical difference. God desires to be close to you all the time, to be your guiding light always. He wants to shine light on every gritty detail of your life. God wants to be your light—that is what the promise of heaven is all about.

Lord Jesus, your light is my guide even when my life and the world seem filled with darkness. Kindle your light in me so that others may see it and be led to glorify you (see Matthew 5:16).

27

Failure Can Help You

He entered Jericho and was passing through it. A man was there named Zacchaeus; he was a chief tax collector and was rich. . . . [Jesus] said to him, "Zacchaeus, hurry and come down; for I must stay at your house today." All who saw it began to grumble and said, "He has gone to be the guest of one who is a sinner." Zacchaeus stood there and said to the Lord, "Look, half of my possessions, Lord, I will give to the poor; and if I have defrauded anyone of anything, I will pay back four times as much." Then Jesus said to him, "Today salvation has come to this house."

LUKE 19:1–2, 5, 7–9

Admitting failure is never easy, but it doesn't have to be devastating. Failure can help you honestly assess and accept your unique combination of gifts, strengths, and limitations. Failure can also help point you in a new direction that you would never have chosen on your own. Facing failure can even help you grow in

55

humility—reminding you of the truth that your value does not lie in what you accomplish but in how much God loves you.

In God's eyes, your "failure" may not even be a failure at all. Perhaps what you learned is invaluable. Failure might be an invitation to grow in fidelity—to be able to persevere in your efforts without any tangible indication of success. This kind of deep faith delights God and allows the Spirit to work freely in you.

Lord, grant me the courage to learn from my failures. Raise me up when I fall, so that I can keep on following you along the way of salvation.

28

God Is with You Always

Jesus came and said to them, "All authority in heaven and on earth has been given to me. Go therefore and make disciples of all nations, baptizing them in the name of the Father and of the Son and of the Holy Spirit, and teaching them to obey everything that I have commanded you. And remember, I am with you always, to the end of the age."

MATTHEW 28:18–20

When Jesus told the disciples at the end of the Gospel of Matthew that he would be with them always, it was not the first time. God reassures his people that he is with them many times throughout the Bible, especially when people feel afraid or unworthy: from Moses (Exodus 3:12), to Jeremiah (Jeremiah 1:8), to the disciples in the New Testament. Jesus promises to be with his disciples—both then and now—in the power and grace of the Spirit.

When you feel incapable or overwhelmed, these divine words are meant to reassure you too. The Spirit can make up for anything you lack or fear. You might feel overawed by the responsibility of raising a child or of making difficult decisions. Perhaps you feel blind to everything except the ways you could fail, or your feelings of inadequacy. But if you spend too much time fretting, you will miss the grace of the Spirit. Remember, God is with you always.

Jesus, because you are with me, I refuse to be afraid today. I make my own the words of Saint Paul: "I can do all things through him who strengthens me" (Philippians 4:13).

29

Find Peace of Heart in Jesus

"Do not let your hearts be troubled. Believe in God, believe also in me. In my Father's house there are many dwelling places. If it were not so, would I have told you that I go to prepare a place for you? And if I go and prepare a place for you, I will come again and will take you to myself, so that where I am, there you may be also."

JOHN 14:1–3

At the Last Supper, Jesus tells the apostles not to let their hearts be troubled. He then tells them that he is the Way, the Truth, and the Life. In other words, if you are willing to make Jesus your Way, Truth, and Life, then you will find peace of heart.

Jesus the Way invites you to imitate the way of love that he lived—to love God, yourself, and others as he does. Jesus is a model to imitate, but he is also much more. He says, "I *am* the Way," not "I show you the way." Jesus is the perfect map; the smoothest, most direct road; the most satisfying rest stop; and the best driving companion—all in one. In everything you experience in your life, every choice you make, Jesus is lovingly present. When you invite Jesus into your life, whether you feel it or not, you will never be alone, because Jesus *is* your journey.

Lord, your tremendous love gives me great joy and peace. I feel safe and secure knowing how much you love me. Following you, I will find true happiness and peace. You are the Way to eternal life.

30

God Delights in Who You Are

But now thus says the LORD,
    he who created you . . .
Do not fear, for I have redeemed you;
    I have called you by name, you are mine.
When you pass through the waters, I will be with you;
    and through the rivers, they shall not overwhelm
        you;
when you walk through fire you shall not be burned,
    and the flame shall not consume you.
Do not fear, for I am with you.

ISAIAH 43:1–2, 5

This passage from Isaiah reveals the Lord's startling attitude to the Chosen People *and* to you—the almighty Creator of heaven and earth doesn't take you for granted but cherishes you and delights in who you are. God sets no conditions for loving you. God doesn't need you to have a good opinion of yourself in order to love you. Even in the darkness of low self-esteem, God loves you.

God knows you better than you could ever know yourself. Your self-image reflects one, or maybe several, aspects of your identity, as a pencil sketch gives an impression of a mountainside. But God doesn't need a sketch. God walks on the mountainside and sees it from every angle, in all its glorious colors and majesty, from every point in time, as you truly are—your inner essence, history, longings, gifts, potential, and your wounds. And God finds you beautiful.

Lord, you know me better than I know myself, and you are always present with me. Help me to see how much you love me, to live in a deeper awareness of your loving presence, and to turn to you in every need.

Prayers

Lord, You Know Me

O LORD, you have searched me and known me.
You know when I sit down and when I rise up;
    you discern my thoughts from far away.
You search out my path and my lying down,
    and are acquainted with all my ways.
Even before a word is on my tongue,
    O LORD, you know it completely.
You hem me in, behind and before,
    and lay your hand upon me.
Such knowledge is too wonderful for me;
    it is so high that I cannot attain it.
Where can I go from your spirit?
    Or where can I flee from your presence?
If I ascend to heaven, you are there;
    if I make my bed in Sheol, you are there.
If I take the wings of the morning

and settle at the farthest limits of the sea,
even there your hand shall lead me,
        and your right hand shall hold me fast.
If I say, "Surely the darkness shall cover me,
        and the light around me become night,"
even the darkness is not dark to you;
        the night is as bright as the day,
        for darkness is as light to you.
For it was you who formed my inward parts;
        you knit me together in my mother's womb.
I praise you, for I am fearfully and wonderfully made.
        Wonderful are your works;
that I know very well.
        My frame was not hidden from you,
when I was being made in secret,
        intricately woven in the depths of the earth.
Your eyes beheld my unformed substance.
In your book were written
        all the days that were formed for me,
        when none of them as yet existed.
How weighty to me are your thoughts, O God!
        How vast is the sum of them!
I try to count them—they are more than the sand;
        I come to the end—I am still with you.

Psalm 139:1–18

God's Love in Christ Jesus

If God is for us, who is against us? He who did not withhold his own Son, but gave him up for all of us, will he not with him also give us everything else? Who will bring any charge against God's elect? It is God who justifies. Who is to condemn? It is Christ Jesus, who died, yes, who was raised, who is at the right hand of God, who indeed intercedes for us. Who will separate us from the love of Christ? Will hardship, or distress, or persecution, or famine, or nakedness, or peril, or sword?

No, in all these things we are more than conquerors through him who loved us. For I am convinced that neither death, nor life, nor angels, nor rulers, nor things present, nor things to come, nor powers, nor height, nor depth, nor anything else in all creation, will be able to separate us from the love of God in Christ Jesus our Lord.

Saint Paul (Romans 8:31–35, 37–39)

God's Dream for Me

Your dream, O Master, is to lay hold of me with
    your divine life.
Your dream is to purify me, to recreate me, to
    make me a new person in your image.

Your dream is to fill me with your love, so that I
love the Father and all my brothers and sisters
just as you do.
Your dream is to draw me to you with the closest
of bonds,
to unite my heart with yours, to make me strong,
to impart to me your divine power
so that I can overcome evil and be constant in
doing good.
Your dream is to inflame me with untiring zeal to
spread your Kingdom.
Your dream is to possess me in this life and in the
life to come.
May your dream come true! May I be able to give
all you ask of me. Amen.

Based on the writings of Blessed James Alberione

"I Am with You"

A Disciple's Dialogue with Jesus Master

I feel alone.	*I am with you.*
I do not understand or see.	*I am your guide.*
I feel unloved.	*I will always love you.*
I feel unimportant.	*I value you always. You are very important to me.*

I feel ignored.	*I hear everything and know everything.*
I feel abused.	*I am your healer and restorer.*
I feel weak.	*I am your strength.*
I feel confused.	*I am your light.*
I feel unwelcome.	*You are always welcome in my presence.*
I feel far away.	*I am always near you.*
I feel unsure.	*I am your surety.*
I don't know.	*I know all.*

Be at peace, my child, I am your All in All!

Jesus, Hold Me Close

My Jesus, hold me close.
Be with me.
Let me lean on You!
Help me discover Who You are for me . . .
and who You are calling me to become.

Marie Paul Curley, FSP

You Are Always Thinking of Me

My God, you are always thinking of me. You are
within me . . . around me. . . . My name is written on the

palm of your hand. May I always and in all things do your will.

Lord, I abandon myself in you and relinquish all worry. I abandon myself completely in you, always.

My God, I want to be hidden in you, to lose myself in you like a drop of water in the ocean.

Venerable Thecla Merlo, FSP

Struggling with Self-Doubt

Lord,
I am struggling with self-doubt again,
not able to hang on
to the dizzying truth
that You love me tenderly,
gently call me,
deeply will my happiness.
Help me to believe,
cherish,
root myself
in Your incredible love.
Help me to recognize Your love in its dailiness,
and allow it to fill me
with joy,

with thankfulness,
with a spirit of truly caring for my loved ones,
and with a love for all Your people that is so vast
    and deep
it will sweep them closer to You.

Marie Paul Curley, FSP

In Times of Anxiety

Father, I know that your love never fails and that you care for everything you have made. Whatever the troubles of our hearts, you guide and sustain us. May the beauty of your creation—the lilies of the field and the birds of the air (see Luke 12:24, 27)—be a constant reminder to me that nothing you have made is ever forgotten.

In moments of fear, give me courage; when I am overwhelmed by anxiety, give me renewed faith in your loving Providence. I ask this through Jesus, your Son. Amen.

Mary Leonora Wilson, FSP

Help Me to Have Perfect Trust

O Christ Jesus, when all is darkness and I feel my weakness and helplessness, give me a sense of your presence, your love, and your strength. Help me to have perfect trust in your protecting love and strengthening power, so that nothing may frighten or worry me, for, living close to you, I shall see your hand, your purpose, your will through all things. Amen.

Saint Ignatius of Loyola

Unfailing Prayer for Hope

Lord Jesus, you see my entire life. You know my thoughts and feelings. You see how hard life can be, how unfair it can seem at times. In all the confusion, one thing is certain: your love for me never changes. I place all my hope in you. Embrace me as I am. Walk with me and guide me. Let me follow where you lead. You desire only the greatest good for me; you are on my side. I place all my hope in you. Help me see how much you want to be part of my life. Teach me to follow you in trust. You are God, my Savior. I place all my hope in you.

Blessing: "May the God of hope fill me with all joy and peace in believing, so that I might abound in hope by the power of the Holy Spirit" (see Romans 15:13).

Mary Martha Moss, FSP

I Believe

I believe . . .
That You are good, gentle and loving, and that You
    love me personally, with a tremendous love.
That You not only want but will my good, and that
    You are with me,
working in me and for me even when I feel so
    alone.
That You are bringing me a future full of hope;
That You lead me on a path that leads to life!
That I can trust Your action, even if not my
    consolation.

Marie Paul Curley, FSP

A Prayer Just for Today

Lord,
    maybe today I just need to try not to doubt
        Your love for me?

As impossible as it seems—is that how You are
    calling me?
Not to doubt You, but . . .
To trust You.
To trust Your goodness.
To trust Your love.
To trust You (even) at work in me.
To trust that You don't make worthless, bad stuff.
To trust . . .
That You love who You make.
That You choose whom You create and sustain.
That Your life and death and resurrection is one
    big "Yes!" to my life, to my meaning, to my
    being loved.

Marie Paul Curley, FSP

BOOKS & MEDIA

A mission of the Daughters of St. Paul

As apostles of Jesus Christ,
evangelizing today's world:

We are CALLED to holiness
by God's living Word and Eucharist.

We COMMUNICATE the Gospel message
through our lives and through all
available forms of media.

We SERVE the Church
by responding to the hopes and needs
of all people with the Word of God,
in the spirit of St. Paul.

For more information visit us at:
www.pauline.org